Aryella,
The Messenger of Fairy Love and Her Fairy Friends

Written and Illustrated by Susan Jane Tilley

Aryella, The Messenger of Fairy Love and Her Fairy Friends

iUniverse books may be ordered through booksellers or by contacting:

iUniverse
1663 Liberty Drive
Bloomington, IN 47403
www.iuniverse.com
844-349-9409

Because of the dynamic nature of the Internet, any web addresses or links contained in this book may have changed since publication and may no longer be valid. The views expressed in this work are solely those of the author and do not necessarily reflect the views of the publisher, and the publisher hereby disclaims any responsibility for them.

Any people depicted in stock imagery provided by Getty Images are models, and such images are being used for illustrative purposes only. Certain stock imagery © Getty Images.

ISBN: 978-1-5320-8397-6 (sc)
ISBN: 978-1-5320-8398-3 (hc)
ISBN: 978-1-5320-8399-0 (e)

Library of Congress Control Number: 2019915065

Print information available on the last page.

iUniverse rev. date: 12/23/2020

Dedication

I am dedicating my first book to my Ascension journey and to my fairies. I thank God for blessing me with creativity and for all the love and abundance in my life. I am so thankful to the day Aryella came into my life and each fairy that came after. They showed me love and helped me see the light and the magic that could be in my life too.

This made me change direction and create this book. I am so happy to share the Love the fairies want to give. I also want to thank my children for all their love and moral support. Always being so positive and caring. I would like to thank my collective family for all their love, light and support. They gave me the pushes I needed to complete this dream. So I could share the love of our Earth Angels with all children and the inner child within us all.

And lastly, thanks to all of my family and friends that supported me. I appreciate all of you! May this book be the first of many, as I and the fairies are so looking forward to sharing all of their love with everyone! I am truly blessed and thankful for this journey.

May everyone also find the key to your happiness!

Love to all,

Susan

Authors Note:

Aryella wants you to know that she is a messenger fairy of Love and wears a heart locket and holds her bracelet with a key in her hand that unlocks the heart to love.

She takes you on a path to meet her fairy friends and as she goes along, she gives you a message of Love.

Please interact with your children and find the messages of love by asking them questions as you journey along with Aryella and her fairy friends. What do you Love? What do you see? What fairy is like you? Do you Love fairies? Do you know more about fairies now? The fairies Love talking with you too!

Remember, our fairies are our Earth Angels and they all have special ways to spread Love and joy to everything. So please have fun as you travel along with Aryella and unlock the Love within your heart!

Aryella, the Messenger of Fairy Love and Her Fairy Friends

Written and Illustrated by Susan Jane Tilley

Hi I am Aryella,

the messenger fairy of love.

I hold
the key
to Love.

Come along with me
and meet my fairy friends.
I will show you how we use
the key to Love.

The sun
and flowers
bring us joy.

2

Hi I am Daisy,
the gardener fairy of Love.

Come dig with me
and I will share
my secret seeds
that grow Love.

Daisy and I Love to garden together,
where we plant seeds of faith, hope and Love.

These are the
best seeds of all.

Hi I am IvyElla,
the glitter fairy
of Love.

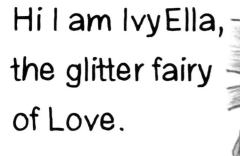

Come climb with me
up my vines,
where I sprinkle Love
with my glitter.

IvyElla and I Love to climb up in the trees
and sprinkle Love to all with IvyElla's glitter.

Glittery Love
makes you smile.

Hi I am Stitch,
the playful fairy of Love.

Come with me
and I will sew my
golden threads
and pull your
hearts to the
Love of fun.

Stitch and I Love having fun, *ha ha,* stitching threads of giggles and having fun with friends.

Stitch fun times together.

Hi I am Joy, the nature fairy of Love.
Come with me and spread joy
to everything with Love.

Joy and I Love being out in nature,
making new friends and sharing Love.

Get out in the river of Love,
where Love swims everywhere.

Hi I am Trevor,
the musical fairy of Love.

Come with me and
tune into the Love
all around you.

Trevor and I Love sending
a song of sweet notes.

tweet love tweet
tweet love tweet
tweet love tweet
tweet love tweet

Music connects
the notes of Love.

Hi I am Willow,
 the dancing fairy of Love.

Come with me and dance
 in the river of Love
 everywhere.

Willow and I Love to dance
in the winds of Love.

Fluttering Love
to every living thing.

Hi I am Clover,
the wishing fairy of Love.

Come with me and
wish all your dreams.
They can come true.
When you Believe!

Clover and I Love catching
princes down at the pond.

It is fun
to make
wishes
of Love.

Hi I am Sawyer,
the strength fairy of Love.

Come build with me
and I will share the tools
that give you Loving strength.

Sawyer and I Love to build friendships.

When we work together
we grow as friends.

I hope you had fun meeting
my fairy friends today
and unlocking your hearts to
the Love around you!

Friends are pieces of Love
that let your heart shine!
We Love You! See you outside!

Printed in the United States
By Bookmasters